BE INTOLERANT

BE INTOLERANT

★ ★ ★ ★ ★

RYAN DOBSON

WITH JEFFERSON SCOTT

Multnomah® Publishers *Sisters, Oregon*

BE INTOLERANT
published by Multnomah Publishers, Inc.

© 2003 by James Dobson, Inc.
International Standard Book Number: 1-59052-152-8

Cover design by Steve Gardner
Cover image of Ryan Dobson by Kristen Haufschild

Unless otherwise indicated, Scripture quotations are from:
New American Standard Bible® © 1960, 1977, 1995 by the Lockman Foundation.
Used by permission.

Other Scripture quotations are from:
The Holy Bible, New International Version (NIV) © 1973, 1984 by International Bible
Society, used by permission of Zondervan Publishing House.
Holy Bible, New Living Translation (NLT) © 1996. Used by permission of Tyndale House
Publishers, Inc. All rights reserved.
Contemporary English Version (CEV) © 1995 by American Bible Society.
Revised Standard Version Bible (RSV)
© 1946, 1952 by the Division of Christian Education
of the National Council of the Churches of Christ
in the United States of America

Multnomah is a trademark of Multnomah Publishers, Inc.,
and is registered in the U.S. Patent and Trademark Office.
The colophon is a trademark of Multnomah Publishers, Inc.

Printed in the United States of America
ALL RIGHTS RESERVED
No part of this publication may be reproduced, stored in a retrieval system, or transmitted,
in any form or by any means—electronic, mechanical, photocopying, recording, or
otherwise—without prior written permission.

For information:
MULTNOMAH PUBLISHERS, INC. • P. O. BOX 1720 • SISTERS, OR 97759

Library of Congress Cataloging-in-Publication Data

Dobson, Ryan.
Be intolerant / by Ryan Dobson with Jefferson Scott.
    p. cm.
ISBN 1-59052-152-8 (pbk.)
1. Church work with youth. 2. Youth—Religious life.   I. Scott, Jefferson. II. Title.
BV4447.D615 2003
239—dc21

                                    2003012459

04 05 06 07 08—10 9 8 7 6 5 4

★ ★ ★ ★ ★

This book is dedicated to Dr. David Noble.
Through his passion for youth he opened my eyes to
Absolute Truth!

Contents

★ ★ ★ ★ ★

Acknowledgments

There are so many people who made this book possible. First and foremost is my family. To my dad, who consistently shows me how to stand against the odds for right and wrong. To my mom, a true prayer warrior, and my sister, Danae, for cheering me on.

I owe endless thanks to the staff at Multnomah Publishers for believing in me and putting up with someone who totally goes against the grain. Special thanks to Don Jacobson, for making me part of your family, and Tiffany Lauer, for putting up with endless calls and harassment.

I couldn't have written this book without Jefferson Scott. Thank you for your tireless work ethic and willingness to learn my language.

To all my friends at Sid's (Sid, Rob, Christopher, Eric, and Sam) for keeping me humble and honest.

To David "PS" Green for all the long talks and forcing me to see things in a different light.

Most of all I want to thank my Lord and Savior Jesus Christ, who to my amazement keeps using me.

I am humbled by this honor. God bless you all.

Ryan Dobson

Thanks to Ryan for his passion about our Christian young people and the deception they're being fed. Thanks to Multnomah for asking me to be part of this project. Thanks to Dr. Steve Lemke and Brian Thomasson for their valuable feedback regarding moral relativism. Thanks to Rod Morris for his moral support. Thanks to Jim Lund for his deft editorial touch. And thanks to my Lord Jesus for bringing the words.

Jefferson Scott

Introduction

★ ★ ★ ★ ★

The Only Way

And Jesus said unto His disciples, "Go into all the world, teaching all men to live any way they want, and urging each to find his or her own path to God. Let not any one of you make someone feel inferior or victimized because of their beliefs. Above all, be tolerant. Verily, verily, I say unto you that what you believe and how you live do not matter, so long as you are sincere."

Leaving that place, Jesus led His disciples to Jerusalem where they broke bread at Club Upper Room. There He addressed them again, saying, "I am one of the ways, one of the truths, and just one possible life. If you are basically a good person, you're okay in my book. And if you choose to come to the Father (or Mother, if you prefer) through Me, that's cool. Now go forth to live according to whatever feels good to you."

And there was much rejoicing.

Which Bible Version Was That?

I promise you won't find that passage of Scripture in any Bible translation. But there are plenty of people today who live as if that's exactly how the Bible *does* read.

In the twenty-first century, everybody wants to be cool with everybody else. Nobody wants to offend others or be thought of as narrow-minded or intolerant. Ours is a live-and-let-live world.

It's tough to be a Christian in that kind of culture, isn't it? You want to follow Jesus. You want your friends to know about Him, too. But whenever you start talking about the Bible and what's right and wrong, everyone jumps up and calls you a judgmental bigot. After all, who are *you* to say what's right or wrong?

And so you keep your mouth shut.

Or maybe you're the kind of Christian who just wants to get along. Jesus promoted a life of peace, right? You're wondering why you can't love Jesus and the next guy love Buddha. The problem with that is you don't fit in with some of your friends because you say you love Jesus— doesn't that name just *freak* people out?—yet you *also* don't seem to fit in with the crowd at church.

If you can relate to what I'm saying, then this book is for you. I wrote it for young people who feel pulled apart by two powerful forces—God and the rest of the world.

"Hello, My Name Is Ryan, and I'm a Speed Freak"

Now before you start hanging with me in this book, you'd better know a few things.

The first thing you should know is that I like speed. Whether I'm on my surfboard in the head-high California surf or dropping in with my skateboard on a twelve-foot vert ramp, I can't get enough of the stuff. My friends tell me I get this crazed look in my eye when I'm surfing. I don't know about that (well, yes I do—they've shown me pictures), but I do know that when I'm flying down a glassy face, hanging on for dear life, I just can't stop laughing. I laugh like a maniac all the way in. Then I paddle back out to the lineup as fast as I can.

The second thing you're going to notice about me is that I'm totally intolerant. **Totally, radically intolerant.** Some people call me a narrow-minded, Bible-thumping, backward-thinking, fundamentalist white male bigot. In fact, it happens every day.

People say I'm intolerant because I speak up when I see something that's just plain wrong. If I find out that a couple of my unmarried friends are having sex, for example, I tell them that what they're doing is wrong.

I also make a habit of standing up and saying that some things are *right*, like loving Jesus Christ with everything in you. People don't like it when I do that, either. I had my tires slashed at least ten times in college. The lifetime guarantee on the tires has paid for itself many times over.

Yeah, I speak my mind about what's right and wrong, but I don't do it to be a jerk. Believe it or not, I do it out of love. If I didn't really care about my friends, I'd let them go on and ruin their lives. The reason I stand up to them is because I love them.

And I'm not intolerant because I get an adrenaline rush from going toe-to-toe with people in open debate. I do it because the love of Jesus flows in me and out from me. If I didn't care about others, I'd just sit down and shut up.

But Jesus doesn't give me that option. He gave up the privileges of His position as the Son of God and did something to help us. It cost Him His life. Most of the people of His day—including religious leaders who should have recognized Him for who He was—refused to follow His teachings. He was rejected, violently opposed, falsely accused, and abandoned in His moment of need. **Out of love for us, Jesus Himself was intolerant**—and He paid the ultimate price to take His unpopular stand. The least I can do in return is suffer a few flat tires.

All right, enough about me.

Time to Get off the Fence

I have one goal for this book. If you're feeling paralyzed in your Christian walk, if you're fearful of what might happen if people find out what you truly believe, I want to take you to a new place where you will gladly stand up for Jesus Christ, no matter what the cost.

I want to bring you out of the darkness of political correctness into the light, peace, and freedom of the truth. I want to take you from hypocrisy to consistency, from moral cowardice to moral confidence. I want to show you that it's not just uncomfortable to be a Christian and be friends with the world at the same time—it's impossible. I want you to speak out for the Lord out of love for your friends.

The truth is out there. And *Jesus* is that truth.

Jesus didn't say He was *one* of the ways to get to God; He said He was the *only* way. When it comes to being intolerant, Jesus is the leader of the pack. He will not let you stay on the fence.

By the end of this book, either you're going to be stoked for Christ or you're going to decide you never really believed in Him in the first place. What do you say? You up for the trip?

Chapter

1

★ ★ ★ ★ ★

An Epidemic of Tolerance

"I did not have sexual relations with that woman."

President Bill Clinton struck a serious pose, pounded the podium, and delivered this declaration with the air of a powerful man who is being detained from serving the American people to deal with trivial details.

The trouble was, he was lying. Not only had he had repeated sexual relations with intern Monica Lewinsky, he lied about it under oath, denied it multiple times on camera, and reportedly encouraged others to lie about it under oath.

What was America's reaction? Lots of people I talked to thought it was great that the President of the United States knew how to have a good time. The poor man worked hard and probably deserved a little action on the side, right?

Under intense pressure and facing impeachment hearings, Clinton finally admitted his lie: "Indeed, I did have a relationship with Ms. Lewinsky that was not appropriate. In fact, it was wrong."

Okay, he said it was wrong. Yet he never seemed all that sorry. Now here's the worst part of it for me: So many young people I know don't think he had anything to be sorry *for.*

Everything's Relative—Or Is It?

Moral relativism. Know what that is? Moral relativism is a way of looking at the world that says what is right or wrong for you depends on what *you* think is morally right or wrong. In other words, everything is relative.

You've heard something like this before, haven't you? "Dude, I know you think that getting high is wrong. Hey, that's cool. Whatever works for you. But I happen to think there's nothing wrong with it, you know? Hang with us if you want. Up to you."

That's the problem with moral relativism—everything's *up to you.*

Bill Clinton is the poster child for moral relativism. He's charming and smart, and he always lands on his feet. He has enlightened opinions on feminism, the environment, war, and social programs. He's accepting and tolerant, and he won't look down on you if you want to break a few rules. Who cares if he lies to the American people and cheats on his wife?

Our former president is a great example of how moral relativism works in our country: If you have politically correct opinions, you can get away with just about anything.

A Tumor on the American Soul

I'm going to play oncologist now and give America an MRI exam. You're going to see that a malignant mass has spread all across our culture.

Where did this disease come from? I'll explain it in one long, run-on sentence: In the beginning everything was great, but then Christianity came and introduced everybody to guilt, and then came the Enlightenment (early eighteenth century), which told us that science and technology could solve everything, but that was even worse because it led to wars and the exploitation of people and the environment, so a few postmodern philosophers decided we are all free to make our own truth and should quit trying to force everyone to believe what we believe and act like we act.

And so moral relativism was born.

What does this disease—this philosophy called moral relativism—look like? Like a TUMOR. Let me spell it out for you.

TOLERANT

In our culture, tolerance is king. We don't want *anybody* to feel bad about themselves. Everybody gets to do whatever they want, and we're cool with it, so long as it doesn't hurt anybody else. And we get to do whatever *we* want, too, and it's nobody's business but our own.

UNTRADITIONAL

What I'm really talking about here are alternative lifestyles. Our generation loves alternative voices, alternative music, alternative medicine—anything, in fact, that flies in the face of "the way things have always been."

It's not just about offending Mom and Dad, though that's a big part of it. I think it's the young person's attempt to show that he (or she) is not just a clone of his parents, but is a unique person who can think for himself. He's throwing out all the old ways because somebody said it was cool and would make him feel powerful.

MARGINALIZED

Our culture loves a victim. If you can show that you've been picked on, pushed around, inconvenienced, or even slightly embarrassed in gym one day, postmodern wisdom says that you have been pushed to the margins of society. You are a good person deserving of a break (especially if the perpetrator was caught on videotape).

Juvenile delinquents are portrayed as victims of a poor

upbringing. The misdeeds of celebrities, athletes, and politicians are quickly forgotten because, after all, they were driven to their sordid behavior by the unreasonable demands of fame and fortune. Look again at Bill Clinton—even after the truth about the Lewinsky affair came out, his supporters never wavered, claiming *he* was the victim of a right-wing conspiracy.

OUTDOORS

Hey, I love the great outdoors, but what we're talking about here is *radical* environmentalism. Many of the same people who defend a woman's right to kill her unborn child would hurl themselves in front of a bulldozer to rescue a nest of spotted owl eggs.

This kind of relativistic thinking says that *people are the problem.* Radical environmentalists believe that humans are to leave the smallest possible footprint on Mother Earth. "Leave the world alone!" they say. "If you can't live in harmony with nature, then you shouldn't live here at all."

REPROBATE

Reprobate means "marked by immorality; deviating from what is considered right or proper or good." Our culture has adopted an "anything goes" morality, a kind of moral *whatever-ness.* Anytime you run into a rule or a traditional moral standard that would keep you from having your fun, you can just say, "I don't believe in a fixed right or wrong. I have the right to explore this path for myself. I believe it's true for me. Try to stop me and I'll scream that my rights are being violated!"

What a deal! Not only are you *allowed* to do whatever feels right, the culture will now come to your aid if someone tries to stand in your way. If you break into someone's house and slip on their floor, you can sue them for thousands of dollars. **Get paid for burglary—what a country!**

Time for Your MRI Exam

Now you know what I mean by a TUMOR. But we're not done with our MRI machine just yet. Let's point this baby a little closer to home. How are *you* doing against the onslaught of moral relativism? Are you holding your ground? Or is the same disease taking hold in your life, too? And what about the people you hang with after class or at church?

Again, let's start with the issue of tolerance. Do you ever find yourself in uncomfortable situations—parties with drinking or drugs, say—where you keep quiet because you don't want to offend anyone? Do your friends, even the ones in your church youth group, walk around saying or wearing things that seem to contradict biblical morality? Is your youth pastor considered a cool guy because he's tolerant and accepting of this kind of stuff?

What about untraditionalism? Are you and your crowd so set on being different or independent that you reject *anything* that conforms to traditional authority? How about your church? There are all kinds of worship styles, but if the window is thrown open to every type of "Christian" faith— to the point where the Bible becomes irrelevant or Jesus is no longer seen as the only way to God—you may get sucked right out that window into a tornado.

Now, our MRI *should* reveal a passion for the marginalized. Jesus Himself has a heart for the outcast and the oppressed. Our God is "father to the fatherless, a defender of widows" (Psalm 68:5, NIV). But when you or your church concentrates only on social programs and food for the hungry, refusing to pass on the good news of the gospel, then your priorities are out of whack. The YMCA is a good example. The *C* in its acronym stands for *Christian*—but I doubt if the people who participate in its programs know it.

Then there is the great outdoors. Maybe you and your friends celebrate "Earth Day." Or maybe you've heard a cry in your church to become more "earth friendly." Remember the "What Would Jesus Drive?" campaign? Don't get me wrong: I think nature is fantastic. I'm out there every chance I get. But I also believe that God placed mankind over nature and told us to subdue it (see the first chapter of the first book of the Bible, verse 28). When we as Christians act like we're not the stewards of nature but rather its servants, I start to get upset.

Do you see any sign of your Christian friends being reprobate—that is, living by the world's anything-goes standards? How about yourself? **I'm not asking if you make mistakes.** Of course you do. But I turn on the TV and see Catholic priests being arrested on charges of pedophilia. I switch channels and see a televangelist living in luxury but crying for more money for his ministry. Then I see some minister get up and defend homosexuality from the pulpit. We're not just talking about mistakes here. We're talking about a deliberate and very unbiblical lifestyle.

The TUMOR Has to Come Out

If an MRI clearly showed a massive growth in your chest sending out cancer cells to every corner of your body, you'd want the thing to come out, right? But just like smokers who won't quit the habit even when they get lung cancer, our patient doesn't want to deal with the problem. **I'm talking about America here.** About today's church. And yes, about you and the guys and girls you hang out with. Like cancer, moral relativism is a life-threatening problem that won't go away by itself. The TUMOR has to come out.

I didn't write this book to fix America. I didn't even write it to change the church. I wrote this book to show *you* that moral relativism and Christianity don't mesh. Have you noticed seeds of this worldly philosophy creeping into your heart? If so, I'm here to help you decide if you want to go the way of the world or the way of Jesus Christ.

It's time to get off the fence, and you've got to come down on one side or the other.

Chapter

2

★ ★ ★ ★ ★

Taking On the TUMOR

A while back, I sat next to an interesting guy on an airplane. Let's call him Josh. When the flight attendants served the meals, they brought Josh a special vegetarian plate.

"Are you a vegetarian?" I asked.

"Yes, I am."

"Why?"

"Animals are my friends," Josh said, in all seriousness, "and I don't want to eat my friends."

I tried really hard not to laugh. I was going to be on the plane with this guy a long time, and I didn't want to get off to a bad start.

Josh and I started talking about this and that. You know, shallow airplane talk. I don't remember what topic we were on, but at one point I said that something was "wrong."

"Oh?" Josh said. "I don't actually believe in right and wrong."

"Really?" I said. "That's very interesting."

Later on, Josh started telling me about the houseboat he lived on. Turns out he'd been subletting a bedroom to a friend. "But I'm going to have to kick him out," Josh said.

"Why are you kicking him out?" I asked.

"Because he's not paying the rent."

"Oh," I said, nodding. "Not paying the rent—that's wrong, isn't it? But wait a sec. I thought you said you didn't believe in right and wrong. Dude, your friend believes that not paying rent is right for him. Who are you to say that what is right for him is actually wrong?" I paused. "Josh, there's no way you can kick him out. You should be tolerant of his beliefs because he's discovered that not paying rent is right for him."

Long, silent pause. I looked over at Josh. He wasn't moving, but I could tell his mind was churning. He was like a car stuck in the sand—spinning his wheels, trying to dig his way out, but not getting anywhere. I did him a favor and broke the silence.

"Josh, you know what? I'm just kidding you. I really think you *should* kick that guy out. Know why? Because what he's doing *is* wrong. He signed a contract promising to pay you rent every month. He stopped doing that. He has broken a contract. Not only is he wrong, but kicking him out is the *right* thing for you to do. It sounds harsh, but it isn't. It's actually showing him mercy, because you're teaching him something important about life, that you can't go along not paying your rent. If he learns that from you, you've given him the tools to have a better life."

Josh saw my point—sort of.

I'd love to tell you that he saw the light on that airplane and asked me what he had to do to become a Christian, but he didn't. At the end of the flight, though, he said something that gave me hope: "I don't know if I consciously believe in right and wrong, Ryan, but maybe I subconsciously believe in wrong."

"Well, that's a start," I said.

Actually, it was way more than a start. For probably the first time, Josh realized that his own life philosophy basically didn't work. You can't recognize that you hold conflicting opinions about something and hang on to both of them for very long. When you start disagreeing with yourself, you're in trouble. Your brain won't let you rest until you get it figured out.

A Philosophy That Disagrees with Itself

Moral relativism doesn't work. It's a broken system, a bankrupt philosophy, a worldview at war with itself. It doesn't even make sense. And the only way people can hold on to it is by not stopping long enough to really think it through.

If you're a Christian and you think there's a way to make moral relativism and biblical Christianity work together, I've got news for you: They won't. Over the next several pages, either I will convince you of the stupidity and corruption of moral relativism, or you're going to be so mad at me that you quit reading this book—and quit calling yourself a Christian.

Let's take this TUMOR out, one chunk at a time.

Taking on Tolerance

Tolerance is the virtue of those who believe in nothing. Rather than stand up for what is right or wrong, the voice of tolerance says we should just let everybody be, that we'll better understand each other and other beliefs and cultures if we accept them as they are.

I can buy that concept—to a point. The question is, where do you draw the line?

Was Hitler wrong to try to kill every living Jew? Of course. Although Hitler believed he was doing the right thing for him and for the Nazi party, even the most tolerant among us would speak out against his reign of terror—if only because he was the very model of intolerance.

Likewise, if you beat up your tolerant roommate, he's probably going to say what you've done is wrong. Or if you steal his wallet. Or if you say you've got a problem with the way he treats his girlfriend. Or, especially, if you go *out* with his girlfriend—even when you tell him that it "feels right for you."

There are actually lots of things (and people) that a moral relativist won't tolerate. It's an intolerant kind of tolerance, you know? It's a system with no right and wrong—except that it's right to believe his way and wrong to believe any other way. He'll tolerate you as long as you're like him. If you don't think, dress, talk, and believe exactly as he tells you, you won't be tolerated.

Of course, the moral relativist doesn't see his intolerance as hypocritical. He hates it when a Christian tries to force his faith on him, but he doesn't mind cramming tolerance down everyone's throats. What is that if not hypocrisy?

Except that if you live in complete opposition to what you say your central belief is, then I say you're more than a hypocrite. You're a liar. One of the foundations of moral relativism is that there is no unchanging standard of right and wrong. And yet the moral relativist lives every day according to a very strict and unchanging set of right and wrong—a rigid code of behavior.

What do you call a philosophy that forcefully and consistently violates its own central pillar of belief?

Broken.

Unstable.

False.

In other words, wrong.

Now let's look at why moral relativism's version of tolerance doesn't fit with biblical Christianity. Would you believe that there are moral relativists in the Bible? Oh yeah, they're everywhere. People doing whatever seems right in their own eyes (see Deuteronomy 12:8 and Judges 17:6). God has always been against that. But would you believe that the Bible talks about some *Christians* who were trying to combine Christianity and moral relativism? It's true. Take a look at 1 Corinthians 5.

The people in the church at Corinth were very tolerant. One of their members was living in incredible sin (sleeping with his father's wife), but they embraced him and his behavior. They accepted his alternative lifestyle.

Sounds like moral relativism, doesn't it? The church members were actually *proud* of their attitude toward this man.

When the apostle Paul found out what was going on, he let 'em have it. He even said he had "decided to deliver such a one to Satan for the destruction of his flesh" (v. 5). No tolerance there. He knew that if the church said *this* was okay for its members, the whole moral structure would collapse into anything-goes morality:

> How terrible that you should boast about your
> spirituality, and yet you let this sort of thing go on.
> Don't you realize that if even one person is allowed

to go on sinning, soon all will be affected? Remove this wicked person from among you so that you can stay pure.

1 CORINTHIANS 5:6–7, NLT

For the Christian, living by today's distorted philosophy of tolerance is impossible. You either think there is an unchanging standard of right and wrong—the Bible—or you don't. You can't hold both opinions at the same time. Either wrong is wrong and must be opposed or wrong is right and should be encouraged. Make up your mind. But here's a word of warning from the Bible:

Woe to those who call evil good and good evil, who put darkness for light and light for darkness.... Therefore, as tongues of fire lick up straw and as dry grass sinks down in the flames, so their roots will decay and their flowers blow away like dust; for they have rejected the law of the LORD Almighty and spurned the word of the Holy One of Israel.

ISAIAH 5:20, 24, NIV

Taking on Untraditional

By untraditional I mean the way moral relativism rejects everything that Christianity and traditional morality stands for. I'm talking about that word again: *alternative*.

Moral relativists don't truly want anything that is unusual or new—because if they did, then Christianity might eventually become an alternative they would have to try. What they really want is anti-Christianity.

If a philosophy is consciously opposed to Christianity, how can a true Christian live by that philosophy? Moral relativism actively rejects the faith of the New Testament and strongly recommends you pick another, more "flexible" belief system.

Moral relativism is untraditional—and since it's traditional in the United States to be pro-American, some take being untraditional to the point of being un-American. Consider Nicholas De Genova, the Columbia University professor who, in the early days of the war in Iraq, called for the defeat of U.S. forces in Iraq and "a million Mogadishus," referring to the *Black Hawk Down* battle in Somalia that resulted in the deaths of eighteen U.S. servicemen. He was so against the war that he actually wanted American military people to be killed. Speaking like a true moral relativist, he said that those Americans who called themselves "patriots" were actually white supremacists.

Back in early 2003, when President Bush was trying to gain support for a war in Iraq, he came under all kinds of fire from the moral relativists in our society. The thing they hit him hardest for was how outspoken he was about his Christian faith. You could understand non-Christians being bothered by that, since so many of them have bought into moral relativism by default. But I think it must've really hurt when he got hit by *Christian leaders* saying he shouldn't be exclusivistic about Christianity.

Look, Jesus isn't one alternative among many. He's not one of the ways to God. **He is the way.** Don't get mad at me—that's not what I said, it's what *He* said: "I am the way and the truth and the life. No one comes to the Father except through me" (John 14:6, NIV).

Christianity isn't one of many valid pathways to God. It's your only option. To disbelieve that is to disbelieve Christianity altogether. If that's where you are, hey, that's your choice. But don't call yourself a Christian.

Jesus divides people. He unites them, too, but when it comes to what you believe, there's no halfway with Jesus. You're either with Him—or against Him. There is no alternative.

Taking on Marginalized

You might be surprised to hear me say it, but I think it is in the love for the marginalized that moral relativism comes closest to Christianity. The Lord has a special passion for the oppressed and the forsaken. Jesus was branded a radical for spending time with those who were considered the outcasts, the undesirables, and the untouchables.

But here's my beef: The folks who follow the moral relativist line are taking it too far. Today, everyone is a defenseless victim. There is no absolute right or wrong, so if I get caught doing something that's against the law (wrong in a legal sense only), it's not my fault. I'll blame it on my parents. Or my boss. Or some traumatic incident twenty years into my past. Or I'll explain that I was "just born that way."

There was the FBI agent who embezzled two thousand dollars and lost it gambling. He got fired. So the ex-agent took the FBI to court, arguing that his gambling behavior was a handicap protected under the Americans with Disabilities Act. He won the case; the FBI was forced to reinstate him.[1]

Anyone who considers himself a Christian should have compassion for the genuinely down-and-out. But it's another story when someone refuses to accept responsibility for his actions and constantly tries to shift blame for mistakes. The Bible says, "If we claim to be without sin, we deceive ourselves and the truth is not in us" (1 John 1:8, NIV).

When it comes to the marginalized "victim," the moral relativist is deceived.

Taking on Outdoors

I don't know how anybody can live with a philosophy that says he himself is the world's problem. That's what moral relativists believe about man's impact on Mother Earth.

Sometimes I think we Christians are intimidated by New Agers when it comes to the environment. We try so hard not to look like wild-eyed ecoterrorists that we stay away from earth-friendly topics altogether. **That's not right.** God created this world as our home and made us its stewards. You can't manage something if you don't even come near it.

But that doesn't mean Christianity and moral relativism are on the same page when it comes to the environment. Most Christians see the environment as a precious gift that we are to subdue and manage. Sometimes that means preservation is the right course of action. Sometimes it means taking the ax to some trees. According to the Bible, the environment is not superior to the needs of men. It's the other way around (see Genesis 1:28–29).

Moral relativism, on the other hand, places nature on a higher plane. We humans should bow in reverence to it and never cut down a tree. The needs of man and of civilization are secondary.

In other words, Christians worship God and manage the earth, while moral relativists worship the earth and disregard God. On the matter of environmentalism, too, Christianity and moral relativism are worlds apart.

Taking on Reprobate

Okay, this is the last letter of our TUMOR. And it's the easiest to talk about.

Moral relativists say that all's fair when it comes to morals. There is no absolute standard of morality. They say that having total freedom from moral restraint is the surest way to happiness. Parties, sex, booze, drugs, whatever else—go for it, dude! Eat, drink, and be merry, for tomorrow we die.

The sad thing is that people who live like this are miserable. They get various chemical rushes or physical pleasures, but they're always brief, fleeting moments. You probably know guys and girls who spend most of their time on a drug or alcohol high. I'm guessing they're not the happiest people on your block.

Why? Because they can't stay on the high. Not only that, but their bodies adjust so that the drugs that got them off last time won't get them off next time. They need more, then more, then *more*. Until they're totally strung out and wasted. Nice life.

To the moral relativist, drug use is not a matter of right or wrong—it's societal. The problem with this for the moral relativist is that there are some things that are always considered wrong in all cultures and all times. Have you ever heard of a culture where murder, adultery, and theft are considered morally right? Could you even imagine such a society lasting very long?

It gets worse for the relativist. The very acts that societies throughout history have branded as immoral are the same ones outlawed in the Ten Commandments. Coincidence? I don't think so. There are unchanging moral laws—the ones laid out in the Bible.

I don't even have to tell you why moral relativism's life of immorality doesn't fit with Christianity. It wouldn't be considered "immoral" if it weren't contrary to the Bible. 'Nuff said.

But I will say that living a moral life is where it's really at. The moral relativist would laugh at that statement, but that doesn't make it untrue. You've seen where the life of immorality leads. A life lived true to the morality of Jesus Christ is full of hope, joy, peace, fulfillment, comfort, and love.

Isn't that what you want? Don't you want an inner tranquility in your soul that stays even when your life gets crazy? Don't you want truth you can build your life on? Don't you want answers to the ultimate questions and substance to fill your deepest emptiness? That's what Jesus offers. But you can't have that and moral relativism, too. They just don't mix.

> "My people have committed two sins: They have forsaken me, the spring of living water, and have dug their own cisterns, broken cisterns that cannot hold water."
>
> JEREMIAH 2:13, NIV

Why do you spend money for what is not bread, and your wages for what does not satisfy? Listen carefully to Me, and eat what is good, and delight yourself in abundance.

ISAIAH 55:2

Moral relativism is a broken cistern (water jug) that can't even hold water. It leaks. It's false bread that promises to fill you up yet can't satisfy your deep hunger.

Imagine looking at a real tumor sitting in a small steel bowl next to the operating table. It's a nasty, black goopy thing, like some kind of cottage cheese creature. One look at it and you're ready to throw up. You can see that it's gross and unhealthy.

I hope that's what you think now of the TUMOR that is moral relativism.

If you're still not sure, keep reading.

Chapter

3

★ ★ ★ ★ ★

A Broken Philosophy

I know a beautiful teenage girl who wears the most revealing stuff you've ever seen. I went with a friend to pick her up one evening. Her dad was out watering the lawn. She came out in something so shocking I couldn't believe it.

I said to my friend, "She's not going out like that, is she?"

He nodded. "Just watch."

She called to her father to tell him she was leaving.

He looked right at her and said, "Have a good time."

When we got to the mall this girl went into the bathroom and changed into modest clothes.

"Dude," I said to my friend, "what's going on?"

"She just wants him to tell her no, but he never does. Next time she'll probably come out nude and he won't even care."

I don't believe people actually want total moral freedom.

It's human nature to want to know where the boundaries are. There's comfort in finding out *This is as far as I can go.* I think people push and push, become more and more outrageous, because they're looking for the walls. They act out to see if someone will finally say, "Okay, that's far enough."

Oh, sure, we complain about not being allowed to do things we think will be fun. But isn't there something comforting about having a consistent moral boundary? It's like watching the lions at the zoo. It's great to get as close as you can so you can check out their big fangs and hear them roar. But isn't it nice to see those steel bars so you know just how close you can go? Without that boundary, the fun can end real quick.

Young people without boundaries often dive into a life of immorality, then find it isn't all they'd hoped for. It's like a mirage in the desert. They keep running for the oasis, but when they get there it's gone.

I think people plunge into this kind of life because it keeps them distracted. Do you have friends in the moral relativist mindset who are constantly listening to music, watching movies, or playing video games? They're probably doing it because they're afraid of what they'll feel if they stop.

Empty. Meaningless. Purposeless.

Moral relativism can't give you hope or peace or answers for life. It sounds good and our culture's digging it right now, but that doesn't change the fact that it doesn't add up.

And so the moral relativist tries to escape. He has to. Because if he realizes his life has no meaning, he's set up for disaster.

That's what's behind the school shootings and suicides and so many other ills in our society. When people decide there are no moral boundaries, that there's no right and wrong, they often conclude that everything is meaningless and they might as well do...whatever.

I love the movie *In the Line of Fire*. John Malkovich plays the ultimate moral relativist. But he's the most miserable kind, because he's smart enough to realize his life is empty and stupid. He decides, since there is no reason not to, to assassinate the president. Clint Eastwood plays the Secret Service man trying to stop him. Clint asks why he wants to kill the president, and Malkovich's answer is the best illustration I've heard of moral relativism's failure: "To punctuate the dreariness."

Ouch. Doesn't that get you?

He has no purpose in his life, so why not kill the president? Why not get himself killed, too? It won't mean anything—nothing will—but at least it'll be interesting for a minute. At least it will punctuate the dreariness.

Moral Relativism Doesn't Work

Moral relativism doesn't follow its own rules, the rules it judges everyone else by. We're tolerant of all—except you, you, and you. There is no standard of right and wrong—except for when you violate what we say is right. You can follow any religion you please—as long as it's on our list of accepted ones. We love to hear alternative voices—but if you try to talk to us about Jesus, we will silence you. We're totally in favor of "anything-goes" morality—unless you use that freedom with my girlfriend, or cut me off in traffic, or steal from me.

It's not just hypocritical, it's fundamentally broken.

Moral relativism just flat doesn't work.

And what about the idea that there is no absolute truth? I mean, first of all, *the statement itself is a declaration of absolute truth.* If you have a moral relativist friend who says, "There is no such thing as absolute truth," he's laying out a truth that he believes will never change. He should put it this way: "It is an absolute truth that there is no such thing as absolute truth." Isn't that crazy? It's self-refuting. It's like me saying, "This sentence does not exist."

So then he says, "Well, okay, but there is only *one* absolute truth, and that is that there is no such thing as absolute truth." But you can't do that. If you can prove one exception to the absolute, it isn't an absolute anymore. If I told you that all ravens were black, but then you produced an albino raven, I couldn't say anymore that all ravens were black. The absolute would be disproved. So, if there is one absolute truth, then you can't say there is no such thing as absolute truth.

If you stop to think about it, plain old common sense is enough to tell you that we rely on absolute truths every day. My name is Ryan. It will be Ryan again tomorrow, and the day after that. When I go surfing, I always find the beach in the same place. The ocean is always to the west of the state of California. That isn't just my reality. It's true for everyone.

Moral relativists like to proclaim the death of absolute truth. But absolute truth is alive and well, and moral relativists count on it every day. Maybe we ought to call it the death of the death of absolute truth. This is just one more pillar of moral relativism that simply doesn't hold up under pressure.

And if all the pillars of a structure can't hold up, maybe you should find an excuse to step outside.

So Why Do People Believe It?

If moral relativism doesn't work, why are there so many moral relativists? That's a very good question.

I like to go rock climbing. If I can't get a rush from speed, then the chance of falling to my death is a good substitute. There's a place I go called Garden of the Gods. People have been climbing there for decades. It has these metal bolts that somebody pounded into the rock years ago. You don't even have to drive your own bolts. Just hook your carabiner in there and up you go.

The problem is that these bolts are so old and have been used so many times that they're not really safe anymore. Some of them are loose. Some are rusted. Some are broken off. But every day people hook their carabiners into those bolts and pretend that if they fall their weight will be held. I call it psychological protection—it's all in your mind.

Don't these guys know it's not safe? Yeah. Don't they realize that today could be the day that this bolt decides to pull loose? Sure. **So why do they do it?**

Because they don't know any other way. Somebody went before and laid out the way they should go, so they're just following. Even though when they stop to think about it they know it doesn't really work and probably can't support them, they depend on those old bolts just the same. How else are they going to get up the hill? They'd have to drive their own bolts or ask for help or find a totally different way up. It's way too hard for most people. It's easier to keep going the way everybody else is going and just hope that today's not the day the bolts come loose.

Moral relativists are a lot like those climbers. They know in their hearts that their life philosophy doesn't work, but they divert themselves with drugs or music or nonstop activity. They are people that deserve our pity. Their whole lives are spent trying to avoid what they subconsciously

already know   that their lives are meaningless and empty.
Yet they keep putting their carabiners in the loose bolts,
hoping they don't fall.

I'm convinced that the reason people buy into moral
relativism is that they're getting something out of it,
something they don't want to give up. Maybe it's the
chemical rush of drugs or alcohol. Maybe it's the thrill of
breaking the rules. Maybe it's the short-lived fun of
commitment-free sex.

It's so sad to think about these people chasing after those
fleeting moments like a kid trying to catch butterflies.
Maybe they catch one now and then, and for that moment
it feels like a good way to live. But most of the time they
miss, and their whole life is focused on catching the next
high—and on avoiding what awaits them in the silence.

It's like the people who keep smoking even when they
know what it's doing to them. Why, if they're not suicidal,
would they intentionally kill themselves? Because they're
getting something out of it. It's transporting them to disease,
embarrassment, and death, but it gives them a little rush
and a little escape today, and that's better than what they get
in the rest of their life.

Sin in a Toga

Moral relativism is not a philosophy you would arrive at
by studying the world around you. If you put something

under your microscope or do real science with your chemistry set or point your telescope at the stars, you will not arrive at the conclusion that there are no constants in the universe. If you study thermodynamics or biology or geology, you will not arrive at anything even resembling the moral relativistic view.

The only way to come up with moral relativism is to begin with an agenda and then look for ways to make your agenda possible. Your starting point is not an observation of the universe, but an action you want to take.

Let's look at some examples. Say you want to have sex outside of marriage. You've decided that, frankly, that's what you want to do. But if you believe in God, you've got a big problem because the Bible says that sex outside of marriage is wrong. What's a body to do?

You've got three options: (1) comply with what the Bible says, (2) do what you want but suffer the consequences, or (3) make up your own philosophy that says God's Word is wrong and sex outside of marriage is right.

Or maybe what you really want to do is live a homosexual lifestyle. Same problem: The Bible says you shouldn't. But hey, if you adopt a philosophy that says there is no right and wrong, then no one can condemn you for living this way.

You see what I mean? Christianity begins with God's

will as revealed in the Bible, and we Christians are supposed to conform ourselves to that. Even science attempts to draw conclusions about how we can best live by studying how the universe works and trying to harness it.

The moral relativist, on the other hand, doesn't want to be conformed to anything. His take is, *If God says I should change, God is wrong. If anyone tries to keep me from living how I want, then that person is narrow-minded and intolerant. I am a good person and my desires are okay just because I have them. Anyone who expects me to change in the slightest is invading my space.*

Moral relativism is sin in a toga. It's selfishness and hedonism and rebellion dressed up in philosophers' robes. Better to rule my own life than have to do what anyone else tells me to do. I am master and creator and lord.

In fact, moral relativism is the same philosophy that Satan used to deceive Adam and Eve. He's still using it today.

Pros and Cons

I won't deny that moral relativism offers a fantastic benefits package to people who buy into it. The more you begin to believe in tolerance as our culture defines it and the more you tell yourself that there is no absolute truth, the better moral relativism begins to look, at least on the surface. After all, it's a much easier way to live. It's the way the world is going. Everybody's doing it.

It's a philosophy that gradually sucks you in. Before you know it, you're considering ideas that would have seemed crazy not too long ago. You hate one of your classes? No one will mind if you skip it once. You want that CD player at the stereo store? It's a big corporation; they won't even miss it. You and your girlfriend want to have sex? It won't hurt anybody.

When you start down this road, you can rationalize just about anything. The operative line is "It's right for me."

Moral relativism makes your life easier in another way: You no longer have to take a stand on anything. Somebody's cheating at school? "Well, that's his business. It doesn't affect me." Your roommate wants an abortion? "I wouldn't do it, but hey, it's her life." Your friend is coming on strong about religion or honesty or loyalty? "Whatever works for you, dude. But it's not my thing, you know? Give me some space."

Moral relativism is also cool because it lets you be kinda-sorta everything. You can have a little bit of Christianity, be a little bit New Age, and throw in some Hinduism and Buddhism. Choose the parts you like. It's like a huge buffet; you can create your own religion with every "kinda-sorta" thing you put on your tray.

When the moral relativist looks at Christianity, he sees

rules and condemnation. Christianity appears to be a giant cold shower. He thinks it's only about sacrifice, following directions, and giving up the "fun" things I just mentioned.

What's the downside of moral relativism? It's an empty existence. It's fun when things are going well, but what does it offer when you're down? Who are you going to lean on when life starts falling apart?

And moral relativism lacks meaning. Purpose. Passion. I mean, what does the relativist have that's worth dying for? He's always looking, but he never finds real joy or peace or rest.

It's an awful way to live.

Of course, the Christian life *is* a harder path. I won't lie to you. Jesus talks about it as the narrow gate and the narrow road (Matthew 7:13–14). Not many even find it, much less walk it. The other road is much wider and you'll have tons of friends there. It's easier to go that way because everybody else is doing it. You can just go with the flow. The problem with that road is it eventually drops you into a pit. If you want eternal life, you have to find the narrow gate and walk the narrow path until the end.

Along the way you'll have love, joy, peace, comfort, hope, and true meaning. You'll really have something worth dying for. Not only that, you'll have something worth *living* for. You'll have true friends, people headed in the same direction as you, sharing the same spirit. You'll never be alone—God's Spirit will be your constant loving companion. You'll find stability and truth and something else moral relativism can never give you: purity.

Have you ever tasted true purity? That thing called holiness? Once you do, once you come close to the flame of God's presence and sense His perfection and His love, you'll want more and more. You'll want to live in that light, to bask in its warmth, to build a house right beside it. You'll want to get as close to that kind of purity as you can get. Because it's better than any of the darkness that this world offers.

If you live the Christian life, you'll have a relationship with the God of the universe. Knowing Jesus is the greatest treasure you could ever discover in this life. He is the only one who will never leave you, no matter what you've done or where you go. He is your heart's true home.

Choose Wisely

I've tried to show you that moral relativism doesn't work. I've tried to show that it doesn't make sense as a philosophy, it denies its own core teachings, and it leaves you miserable and alone.

You just can't be a moral relativist and a Christian at the same time. That's like being dead and alive at the same time.

Now, sometimes I have days when I feel like that, but you know what I mean!

The real truth is found in the Bible. If you can tell me how it's biblically correct to reject Christianity as the only way to God and say that all religions are equally valid, I'd love to hear it. And if you can show me in the Bible how it's okay with God for you to sin, I'd be all ears.

But you can't. Nobody can.

Maybe you started reading this book thinking you could be kinda-sorta a moral relativist and kinda-sorta a Christian. I hope by now you realize that you can't. They're mutually exclusive.

> Stay away from people who are not followers of the Lord! Can someone who is good get along with someone who is evil? Are light and darkness the same? Is Christ a friend of Satan? Can people who follow the Lord have anything in common with those who don't?
>
> 2 CORINTHIANS 6:14–15, CEV

You've got one foot on a train to Florida and the other on a train to California. They're going to tear you apart if you don't jump onto one or the other.

Which will it be?

Chapter

4

The Case for Biblical Christianity

In the beginning, God created the heavens and the earth. God was immediately hit with a class action suit for failure to file an environmental impact statement. God was granted a temporary permit for the project, but was stymied with the cease and desist order for the earthly part.

Then God said, "Let there be light!"

The officials demanded to know how the light would be made. Would there be strip mining? What about thermal pollution? God explained that the light would come from a large ball of fire. God was granted provisional permission to make light, on the conditions that no smoke would result from the ball of fire and that He would obtain a building permit. To conserve energy, He had to have the light out half the time. God agreed and offered to call the light "Day" and the darkness "Night." The officials replied that they were not interested in semantics.

God said, "Let the earth put forth vegetation, plants yielding seed, and fruit trees bearing fruit" (Genesis 1:11, RSV).

The EPA agreed, so long as only native seed was used.

Then God said, "Let the waters bring forth swarms of living creatures, and let birds fly above the earth" (Genesis 1:20, RSV).

The officials pointed out that this would require approval from the Department of Game, in coordination with the Heavenly Wildlife Federation and the Audubon Society.

Everything was okay until God said the entire project would be completed in six days. The officials said it would take at least two hundred days to review the applications and the impact statement. After that there would be a public hearing. Then there would be ten to twelve months before they would even consider...

At that point God created hell.

A Reason for the Hope That Is in You

I hope you're laughing with me here. It's pretty bad when God Himself isn't tolerated by the tolerance brigade.

Since you're still reading, my prayer is that you're now falling off the fence—in the right direction! By the end of this chapter, I want you all the way down on Jesus' side of that fence.

More than that, I want you not only to be sure that you're following Jesus with all your heart, but to be able to go out there and tell your friends why you believe what you believe. I want to give you some answers for their hard questions. In this chapter I want to give you the tools "to make a defense to everyone who asks you to give an account for the hope that is in you" (1 Peter 3:15).

But First...

Let's say that when you started reading this book, you were trying to live as an "inclusive Christian." Some people in this position would just go right over to being a Christian all the way. I hope that's what you do. I hope you become a Christian who takes the Bible seriously and believes that Jesus really is the only name given under heaven by which people can be saved.

But I know that some people won't go that route right away. Maybe they've got something they're not quite willing to let go of—like a sexual relationship with someone, or a borderline addiction. What they'd really like to do is find some other belief system that will still let them do that thing or stay in that relationship.

If that's you, I have to give you a little challenge. You can't be a Christian *and* anything else—not a Hindu, not a Taoist, not a Hare Krishna. No other religious belief system or hedonistic philosophy can work alongside Christianity. It's all about what C. S. Lewis said: *Mere Christianity.* Christianity all by itself.

Because only Christianity—only the *Christ* of Christianity—can take away your sins, fulfill your deepest longings, heal those buried hurts, and bring you into heaven. Other beliefs do for your eternity what mixing water into your gas tank will do for your car: get you stranded in a hurry.

Three Absolute Truths

I'm not going to spend any more time arguing for absolute truth. I'm just going to assume that you and I agree it exists and move on to the three absolute truths you *absolutely* need to believe if you're going to be a biblical Christian:

1. The Bible is the true and inspired Word of God.
2. God exists and is exactly as the Bible describes Him to be.
3. Jesus is the only way to get to God.

Absolute Truth #1: The Bible Is the True and Inspired Word of God

If I can prove that the Bible is divine in origin, wouldn't that mean that everything in it is true? And what do you find in it except the other two absolute truths: that God exists, exactly as the Bible describes Him, and that Jesus is the only name given under heaven by which people can be saved? Proving the Bible to be of divine, suprahuman origin is the linchpin, so I'll start there.

The key is prophecy. The Old Testament lays out 332 distinct prophecies or predictions about the Messiah, Jesus Christ. These include the place, time, and manner of His birth; His betrayal by a trusted friend; the manner of His death, suffering, and burial; and hundreds more. All 332 were *literally fulfilled* in Jesus.

Okay, anybody can write predictions about things that might happen thousands of years in the future. It's safe to do that because no one here will be alive to find out if you were right or not.

So let's say you made these predictions and they lasted for a thousand years and people wanted to read them because they thought you had some supernatural powers of prediction. Nostradamus, anyone? Then the question would be: Were you right? Now, if you were smart, you'd do what Nostradamus did over four hundred years ago (and what horoscopes and fortune cookies do today)—you'd write in superfuzzy terms. It might read something like this:

> A man with amazing abilities will travel to a far land
> and bring back a terrible beast. All will be
> astonished and call his name Marvelous. Then the
> great group of power will go to war against the
> branch that had fallen, and there will be a famine.

Yada yada yada.

Gullible people would be able to find good fits for all of your symbols and suddenly you would be famous. Dead, but famous.

What you'd definitely want to stay away from if you were planning this are *specifics*. Do not give specific information in your predictions, things like locations, detailed events, or precise sequences. Those will show you as a fake right away. I mean, how dumb would it be to say in exactly X years a boy child will be born in this specific town to parents from this specific family? His birth will be amazing because he will be born of a virgin. He will be killed prematurely by being hung on a wooden execution device. He will be spit on in his death. None of his bones will be broken. He will be killed alongside criminals and buried with the rich.

And after that, he will rise from the dead.

Dude, those are *totally* the wrong kind of things to predict if you want to stand a chance of being right. You've got to be more generic. Specifics will kill you.

But that's exactly what the Old Testament does. It contains more than three hundred specific predictions about the birth, life, death, and resurrection of the Messiah—all made hundreds of years before His birth.

The only two reasons I can think of that you'd ever make such explicit and unambiguous predictions are: (1) you're wrong and you know it but you don't care because you'll be dead when people find out, or (2) you're right and you know it and you don't mind taking God at His word and writing it down exactly as He tells you to.

We don't have time to look at all 332 prophecies, so let's pick a few to concentrate on. Let's just look at the predictions surrounding one portion of the Messiah's life: His betrayal.

Psalm 41:9 says, "Even my close friend, whom I trusted, he who shared my bread, has lifted up his heel against me" (NIV). That last phrase means to rebel against or to betray.

That's pretty detailed, isn't it? King David was being mighty reckless to write out such specific predictions. He was violating the first rule of making predictions. But maybe he believed his prophecies. Let's see if it was fulfilled in the life of Jesus.

Judas was one of Jesus' disciples. He was one of the Twelve, counted among Christ's closest friends, one of His daily companions for at least three years. Judas was especially trusted—he was the one allowed to carry the money for the group (John 13:29). When Jesus ate his last early meal, Judas was there.

David's prophesy was on the money. In fact, Jesus Himself spoke of this prophecy in front of the disciples just before it was fulfilled (see John 13:18).

Let's look at another passage in the Old Testament. The prophet Zechariah predicted that the Messiah would be betrayed for thirty pieces of silver (Zechariah 11:12). Did it come true? Yes. When Judas left Jesus, he went to the chief priests and offered to give Him over to their power. He offered to lead their soldiers right to Him and even to show which one was Jesus. For his troubles, they paid him…you guessed it. Thirty pieces of silver (Matthew 26:15).

Thirty pieces of silver. That's pretty specific. I mean, what if they'd paid in copper or had given him fifty pieces? Then Old Testament prophecy would've been wrong. But it wasn't.

What happened next? Well, when Judas realized what he had done, he tried to give the money back. He took it to the chief priests and threw it at their feet (Matthew 27:3–5). But it was blood money, so the priests used it to buy a potter's field to bury strangers who died while in Jerusalem (v. 7).

Would you believe that's in the Old Testament, too? In Zechariah 11:13, we learn that he took the thirty pieces of silver and threw it to the potter. Get it? He gave the betrayal money to the potter, which is what the chief priests did with Judas's blood money when they paid the potter for his field.

The fulfillment of Old Testament prophecies doesn't end there. David predicted that the betrayer would meet an untimely death for his treachery (see verses 15 and 23 of Psalm 55). What did Judas do after he'd betrayed Jesus and tried to return the money? He went out and hanged himself (Matthew 27:5). He's dead less than twenty-four hours after his betrayal—that's pretty untimely, I'd say.

Okay, so hundreds of years before Jesus was even born, godly men wrote down prophecies of what would happen to the Messiah. We've only looked at the ones related to his betrayal, and already it's an impressive "coincidence" that these things could have come true in the life of one man. What are the odds that even this handful of prophecies could have been just the luck of a couple of ancient writers?

Way back in 1958, a scientist named Peter Stoner tackled that very question. In a famous little book called *Science Speaks*,[2] Stoner looked at the probability that just 8 of the 332 predictions of the Messiah could've been coincidentally or accidentally fulfilled in one man, much less a man who actually proclaimed Himself to be the Messiah. He looked at the probability of each of the eight individually, and then added up the probabilities for all eight.

His mathematical conclusion, verified by the American Scientific Affiliation, was that the chance of all eight being accidentally fulfilled in one man was 1 in 10^{17}. That's a 1 in 100,000,000,000,000,000 chance of it being coincidental.

Even the lotto gives you better odds than that! You've got a 1 in 18,000,000 chance of winning the California Lottery. I'm no statistician, but I'd bet that you'd have better odds of winning the California Lottery *every time you played* than having eight of these prophecies fulfilled in one man.

To help us even grasp such a small probability, Stoner came up with this illustration. Take 100,000,000,000,000,000 silver dollars and lay them out across the state of Texas. They would cover the entire land surface of the Lone Star State two feet deep. Now mark one of these silver dollars—paint it red—and toss it into the stack. Mix it up real good. Finally, blindfold a guy and tell him he can walk across the state as far as he wants, but then he's got to bend down and pick up just one silver dollar. And it has to be the red one on the first try.

That's how likely it is that eight messianic prophecies could've been randomly fulfilled in anyone, much less the one who claimed He really was the Messiah.

Multiply this out to 332 Old Testament predictions that were precisely fulfilled in Jesus Christ, and what do you have?

You have proof of the divinity of Old Testament prophecy.

So if there was a divine hand behind the prophecies that referred to and were fulfilled in Jesus Christ, doesn't it make sense that there was a divine hand behind the rest of the Bible? And if the things the Bible said about Jesus were objectively proven to be true and accurate, wouldn't it be fair to conclude that the rest of what the Bible says is just as true and accurate?

The Bible is the divine and true Word of God. What it says is true.

If that is so, then it happens to also prove the other two absolute truths I mentioned earlier. How can I say for sure that God exists and is exactly as the Bible describes Him? Because the Bible—which we have just agreed is divine, trustworthy, and true—says so. How can I say that Jesus Christ is the only way to get to God? Because the Bible says so.

If you're going to make it out there as a Christian in this culture, you're going to have to believe with all your heart that the Bible is true. Everything hinges on it.

Absolute Truth #2: God Exists and Is Exactly as the Bible Describes Him to Be

I saw a book cover once that showed the throne of God with a Santa Claus hat lying on it. Our culture would love to transform God into Santa—a gentle, forgiving deity who winks at sin and lets everyone into heaven just 'cuz. We want to make God into our image.

But the truth is that *we* are made in God's image, not the other way around. He is creator, sustainer, initiator, and completer. He holds everything and everyone in His hand. And since He made the clubhouse and created the members, He gets to set the rules.

Who is the God of the Bible? He has scores of attributes we could talk about, but to me they all boil down to two— *love* and *holiness*. He is loving and forgiving, as our culture says, or else He never would've sent Jesus to redeem us and reconcile us to God. His love is seen in His patience, His grace, and in the good gifts He loves to shower on His children.

But He's not Santa Claus. He is also holy. This is the side moral relativists don't like. He is the divine Judge. He points at sin and calls it evil. He can be stern and full of wrath. And at the end of time, He will finally shut the door, and no one else will be allowed to enter the kingdom. Those who rejected His holiness in life will not have their rebellion winked at and brushed aside. They will go into hell for eternity.

You can't understand God without seeing both these attributes—love and holiness—constantly working together. It was holiness that expelled Adam and Eve from the Garden, but love that even in that moment promised a redeemer (Genesis 3:15). It was holiness that caused God to turn away from His own Son when Jesus was on the cross bearing the sins of the world; but it was love that had sent Him there, love that held Him there, and love that raised Him from the grave.

God hasn't hidden Himself.

He wants to be known. Even people living in a time or place untouched by Christianity can see God in creation (Romans 1:19–20) and in their conscience (Romans 2:15). He has revealed Himself through the Bible and through His acts and words.

Even non-Christians know that certain things are right and other things are wrong. It's one of God's fingerprints on our lives, one of the things that shouts to our hearts and minds that a good and morally unchanging God is really there.

God's ultimate revelation of Himself was in Jesus Christ. Think about this: If the God of the Bible was to somehow become a person, what would you expect that person to act like? In his book *Evidence That Demands a Verdict,* Josh McDowell made this list of what we'd expect God-in-a-person to be like. We'd expect Him to:

1. Have an unusual entrance into life,
2. Be without sin,
3. Manifest the supernatural in the form of miracles,
4. Have an acute sense of difference from other men,
5. Speak the greatest words ever spoken,
6. Have a lasting and universal influence,
7. Satisfy the spiritual hunger in man, and
8. Exercise power over death.[3]

Well, what do you think? Does that describe Jesus? To this list I say: virgin birth, yes, yes, yes, oh yeah, absolutely, definitely, and way yes. If you want to know what God is like, you don't have to look any further than Jesus Christ in the Bible (see John 14:8–11 and Colossians 2:8–10).

God exists and is exactly how the Bible depicts Him to be.

Absolute Truth #3: Jesus Is the Only Way to Get to God

Jesus is the only way to God.

That's about as narrow, intolerant, and exclusivist as you can be. It says that all other religions aren't just inferior, but are wrong. It's a slap in the face to every Hindu-Buddhist-New-Ager-Whatever belief system.

But if the other two absolute truths are true, then there's no way around this one, either. If the Bible is the true Word of God, then everything in it is true. And the Bible says that

Jesus is the *only* way to get to God. Take a look at these verses:

- "Jesus said to him, 'I am the way, and the truth, and the life; no one comes to the Father but through Me'" (John 14:6).
- "Jesus said to her, 'I am the resurrection and the life; he who believes in Me will live even if he dies'" (John 11:25).
- "This is the will of My Father, that everyone who beholds the Son and believes in Him will have eternal life, and I Myself will raise him up on the last day" (John 6:40).
- "For Jesus is the one referred to in the Scriptures, where it says, 'The stone that you builders rejected has now become the cornerstone.' There is salvation in no one else! There is no other name in all of heaven for people to call on to save them" (Acts 4:11–12, NLT).

No other name but Jesus gets you to heaven. Not Buddha, not Muhammad, not Joseph Smith, not Mary Baker Eddy, not Krishna, not L. Ron Hubbard, not Gandhi, not Abraham, not the pope, not Mother Mary, not Confucius, and not the Dalai Lama. Talk about narrow!

But that's just it. It's supposed to be narrow. Jesus said:

"Enter through the narrow gate; for the gate is wide and the way is broad that leads to destruction, and there are many who enter through it. For the gate is small and the way is narrow that leads to life, and there are few who find it."

MATTHEW 7:13–14

Sometimes there really is just one right way to do something. So if the Bible is true, as we've seen, and if Jesus is the Son of God, as the Bible says, and if Jesus says that He really is the only way to get to God, then we have to say it's true. We don't have any other options. And if it's true that there's no other way to get to God but Jesus, then every other way is wrong. You with me?

If every other way that people use to try to get to God is wrong, then what is the most loving and kind thing to do for them? Is it to just let them go on living in ignorance and misery, even though you know they're wrong and you have the truth that would save them?

It's actually an act of *love* for a Christian to stand up and say, "You know what? What you're doing and what you believe is wrong. Let me talk to you about why I say that." Yes, it's narrow, and yes, it's intolerant. But if it's true, then maybe that's the risk you take. Out of love.

Jesus is the only way to get to God.

Liar, Lunatic, or Lord

Have you ever heard anybody say, "Oh, I believe in Jesus—I believe He was a great moral teacher, like Buddha and Gandhi"? Most likely that person is trying to be tolerant. He doesn't want to dis Jesus and Christianity—or any other religion, either.

But Jesus doesn't leave us with the option of tolerating all religions. If He had uttered only good moral teachings, then you could say He was just a good moral teacher. But if that's all He was trying to be, He totally blew it, because He said things way beyond simple moral teaching.

He said He was God.

> Then the high priest asked him, "Are you the Messiah, the Son of the blessed God?" Jesus said, "I am, and you will see me, the Son of Man, sitting at God's right hand in the place of power and coming back on the clouds of heaven."
>
> MARK 14:61–62, NLT

Jesus said this kind of thing over and over. Another time, when He was being questioned by the Jewish religious leaders, He said it as plainly as it can be said: "I and the Father are one" (John 10:30). On His last night with His disciples, Jesus said it again: "He who has seen Me has seen the Father" (John 14:9).

Jesus claimed to be God.

Therefore we can't think of Him as just a good moral teacher anymore. Why not? Because once you start making claims like that, you'd better be able to back them up. (C. S. Lewis developed this whole argument,[4] and I love it.)

Jesus said He was God—so what are you going to do about it? You really only have two options: You have to say His claims were either true or false.

Let's start with the moral relativist's answer: His claims were false. He wasn't God. All right, then you're left with only two conclusions, neither of which is that He was a good moral teacher. If a man repeatedly and publicly spouts a major untruth, he can't be a good moral teacher. You have to say He was either a liar or a lunatic.

If you say that Jesus was a liar, you've got some problems. First, you've been calling a liar a good moral teacher, so your own thinking has been wrong. Second, if He knew His claims were false and yet you deliberately foisted them on gullible people, that makes Him a hypocrite because He denounced liars in His ministry. He said that those who lie are children of their father, the devil (John 8:44), which would make Him a child of the devil, too. See where we've gotten? If Jesus told such a bold and hypocritical untruth, then He was a liar, and by Jesus' own definition those who breathe out lies are demon spawn.

Are you ready to say that Jesus was a demon?

No? Then let's look at the other option: Jesus' claims were false but He didn't know it. He was deluded. He sincerely believed He was God, but wasn't. He was nuts. I like what C. S. Lewis says here. If Jesus were a lunatic, He would be "on the level of a man who says he is a poached egg."[5]

Okay, but if Jesus were that fuzzy-headed, how could the rest of His teachings be so sane and coherent? How could He build an entire theological system and communicate it as an unchanging entity over a span of at least three years if He was seriously delusional? Can you see His madness in the calm authority of His teachings? Can you see it in the mild and practical spirit of His lessons or the clarity and simplicity of His language?

Historian Peter Schaff wrote this in a tract called *The Person of Christ*:

Is such an intellect—clear as the sky, bracing as the mountain air, sharp and penetrating as a sword, thoroughly healthy and vigorous, always ready and always self-possessed—liable to a radical and most serious delusion concerning His own character and mission? Preposterous imagination![6]

If Jesus said He was God but wasn't, then He was either a demonic liar or a mistaken lunatic. Are you ready to call Him either one? If not, what's left? Only one thing. If Jesus said He was God and it's impossible that that claim was false, you're pretty much forced to say His claims were true.

He was and is Lord.

You do have a choice left to you, though, even now. Even if Jesus really is God, as He said, you can still choose to accept or reject Him. He wants to have your whole heart. He gave all of His for you. In return, He'll give you meaning, joy, peace, hope, companionship, supernatural power for this life, and entrance into the next. **But the choice is up to you.**

You can reject all that if you want, but what you can't do is stay on the fence about Him. Either His claims were true or they weren't. If they were true and Jesus really is the only way to get to God, what are you going to do about it?

So What?

We've looked at three absolute truths. I've attempted to show that they're true and why it's important that they're true. But one question remains: What does it mean to your life?

How does it impact your life that the Bible is really the true and divine Word of God? How does it change anything that God really exists and is exactly as the Bible describes Him? And what difference should it make that Jesus truly is the only way to get to God?

First, if the Bible is really true, how should that impact your life? I guess the most obvious answer is that you ought to begin allowing your life and thinking to be shaped by what the Bible says. That means taking the time to read it, in a translation that clicks for you, on a daily basis. You read it, you think about it, maybe you memorize a piece of it now and then. And before you know it, it's starting to transform you from the inside out. That is what the Christian life is all about (Romans 12:2). You take your marching orders from what God says in the Bible.

Trust me, it'll rock your world.

Second, if it's true that God exists and that He's exactly how the Bible says He is, how should that affect your life? For one, it ought to make you take sin seriously. If God really is holy, then He hates sin. He can't even have it near Him. So if you've got unconfessed sin running rampant in your life, He can't be near you, either. You've got to get that taken care of by confessing it to Him (1 John 1:9).

And if God is who the Bible says He is, then He's this giant loving daddy. That ought to change your life. He does still discipline His children like a good father would, but God isn't some angry judge just waiting to smite thee. He's a loving father who delights to give His children what they desire. So climb up into His lap and lean on back for a bit.

It's a Leap

In the end, all philosophies and belief systems are based on faith. Even science is based on faith. It takes pure faith, for example, to believe that humans evolved from fish. And what is atheism but the *belief* that there is no God? Moral relativism is the same way. You've got to *believe* that there is no such thing as absolute truth and all the rest. **Christianity, too, is based on faith.** But if you're going to put your faith in something (and you are, whether you realize it or not), then shouldn't it be something that works on all levels? Christianity offers everything I've mentioned already—love, joy, peace, comfort, purity, hope, passion, and so much more. Jesus is there for you when you're up, and He doesn't abandon you when you're down. Christianity isn't based on your good works, as so many other religions are, but on God's good works on your behalf.

Christianity also offers the one thing no other faith system can provide: meaning. I'm talking about true meaning, that ultimate sense of soul-rightness that says, "This fulfilled life, this relationship with the living God, is what I was born for." When you live for Christ, you fit into His larger purpose for each member of His family—to rest in the care of the Good Shepherd and to lead others into the flock as well.

> God...reconciled us to himself through Christ and
> gave us the ministry of reconciliation: that God was
> reconciling the world to himself in Christ, not
> counting men's sins against them. And he has
> committed to us the message of reconciliation. We
> are therefore Christ's ambassadors, as though God
> were making his appeal through us. We implore you
> on Christ's behalf: *Be reconciled to God.*
>
> 2 CORINTHIANS 5:18–20, NIV, ITALICS MINE

So how do you do that? How do you step out into a
culture gripped by moral relativism and tell them that
they're wrong—but do it in a way that leads them to Christ?
That's what we're going to talk about next.

Chapter

5

★ ★ ★ ★ ★

How to Be Intolerant— In Love

On May 26, 2002, a towboat on the Arkansas River in Oklahoma accidentally pushed a barge into a concrete bridge support. The bridge was where Interstate 40 crossed the river. At the impact, a third of the bridge collapsed.

The problem was that people on the interstate couldn't see that the bridge was out. Fishermen in boats below watched in horror as car after car shot off the edge of the bridge at seventy miles an hour, plunging sixty-two feet to the river. Three eighteen-wheelers went over, along with seven passenger cars, including one carrying James and Misty Johnson and their three-year-old daughter, Shea.

The fishermen immediately began pulling survivors out of the water. But meanwhile cars kept dropping into the river. When they pulled a truck driver out of the water, he shouted, "Somebody stop the cars!"

So fisherman Alton Wilhoit grabbed a flare gun from his boat and ran up to the interstate, where another semi was headed for the bridge. Wilhoit fired the flare—it struck the truck right on the windshield.

The driver slammed on the brakes. The wheels locked up and the trailer came to a stop with the truck's front wheels hanging over the ledge. The driver threw it into reverse and pulled away, effectively blocking the road and warning other drivers.

Fourteen people died that day, including precious Shea and her parents.[7] But how many more would've died if Alton Wilhoit hadn't done what it took to warn the people who were blindly headed toward their death?

Load Your Flare Gun

You and I can be Alton Wilhoits for the world. We know the bridge is out. We know that people are naively accelerating to their deaths. And we're in the right place at the right time with the right tools to do something about it. **Your friends are about to go over the edge.** People in your family are about to go over the edge. Our whole country is about to go over the edge. They don't know it. They don't see any sign of it. But that doesn't change the fact that it's true.

Moral relativism is like that Oklahoma interstate. It's a road that seems to offer an easy journey, smooth driving all the way. Except that when you least expect it, the joyride turns into a terrifying plunge with no escape.

Someone's got to tell people that the bridge is out. They may not like it. They may complain that other roads don't give them the freedom this one gives. They may even mock you, abuse you, and try to run you down for saying their way is wrong. But does that somehow fix the bridge? And if they call you a bigot and tell you to leave—or if you're just pretty sure they would—are you excused from warning them? Would it be okay for you to just find a good seat to watch the cars go flying?

Telling people that moral relativism is wrong and Christianity is right isn't about being judgmental or spoiling anyone's fun or favoring rules over the free expression of one's personal idea of right and wrong. It's about being a hero. A rescuer. The person who will go to any length to save people from a disaster they don't see coming.

I hope that's what you want to do now. You've seen that it's impossible to be a moral relativist and a Christian at the same time. But I'm sure you know lots of people—maybe even family and friends—who are trying to do just that. They need to be warned! It's no secret that the world around you is headed down that same interstate. Maybe there's something you can do about it.

That's what we'll deal with in this last chapter: how to step in front of the "cars" racing toward destruction and launch a flare. It's definitely not tolerant. You'll be saying that their way is wrong and dangerous. The idea is to do it in a way that leads people to Jesus. You have to learn how to be intolerant—in love.

Here's a five-phase plan for doing that.

Phase 1: The Prayer Closet

Isn't that a funny term? Like you have a coat closet, a linen closet, and a prayer closet? Do you keep your prayers folded? Surrounded by cedar? Hung on hangers? What I mean by "prayer closet" is the private time you have with God.

Everything starts here. Before you can go out into the world to warn anyone of anything spiritual, you need to have your own spirit settled on God. Jesus said, "Out of the overflow of the heart the mouth speaks" (Matthew 12:34, NIV). In other words, what comes out of your mouth is what's in your heart.

That's always the first thing I think when I hear people cussing. They say those words with their lips because that's what their hearts are full of. We all say with our lips what's in our heart—especially when we're under pressure. So if you want to be sure you speak the words of God with your lips, you'd better have the Word of God in your heart.

Are you having a daily quiet time? I challenge you to do it. You want to live the

Christian life all the way, right? Well, this is part of it. If you're not willing to give a little bit of time to the most important thing a Christian does every day, then maybe you're not ready to follow Jesus all the way after all. I told you, it's not the easy road. But the easy road leads to a collapsed bridge, remember?

Get up fifteen minutes earlier. Grab your Bible (make sure it's a translation you understand—the *New International Version, New Living Translation,* or *New American Standard* are really good ones). Pick a place in the Bible to read (if you're just starting out, try reading in the Gospel of John). Read for seven minutes or so. Then for the rest of the time think about what you read, open your spiritual ears for God to speak to you, and pray.

Don't get hung up on reading a whole chapter or a certain number of pages. Just read until something strikes you. I once heard a teacher say that you should keep reading until you can't help but start jotting down notes. I like that. But what you're looking for—listening for, really—is God's message to you for that day. His Spirit *owns* the Bible and He will make His personalized instructions leap off the page to your eye when you read it.

That's why it's so important to be reading the Bible every day—it's the main way God communicates with you. You wonder why He doesn't ever speak to you verbally? It's because He's already said everything He needs to say! It's written down in the Bible.

The Bible talks about spiritual armor (Ephesians 6). What you're doing by reading your Bible each day is suiting up in your armor. I know people who like reading their Bible at the end of the day instead of the morning. Hey, that's cool, as long as you're reading every day. But for me that always feels like I'm suiting up *after* the battle. I read the Word and go, "Oh, *that's* what I should've done!" But as long as you're putting the Word of God into your heart daily, I don't think God cares when you do it.

What you read tonight will be in your heart for tomorrow.

Here in this stillness is where God really does open-heart surgery on you. It's where He transforms you. It's where you come face-to-face with the God of the universe. It's an awesome, inspiring time. And everything springs from it. This is the crux of the Christian life: spending time with the lover of your soul. This is where you come to understand what it means to have a personal relationship—a friendship, even—with Jesus Christ. It's the time to ask Him how you can serve Him and fit into what He's doing in the world. It's the time to worship Him.

> "Come to Me, all who are weary and heavy-laden, and I will give you rest. Take My yoke upon you and learn from Me, for I am gentle and humble in

heart, and you will find rest for your souls. For My yoke is easy and My burden is light."

MATTHEW 11:28–30

I can't emphasize enough how important this daily time is. Without it, you are powerless, drained, and ineffective, like a branch that's not connected to the tree anymore (see John 15).

Phase 2: The Home Team

In a real war, Rambo gets killed. The guy who goes it alone, single-handedly taking on the enemy, provides a sweet target for the bad guys to concentrate their firepower. "I am an army of one" is, after all, just a recruiting slogan. Once you enlist, you find out that it's all about the team.

The same is true in Christianity. If you try to take on the culture of our day by yourself, you're going down in a hurry. It's true that one day you will be called upon to stand alone for what you believe in, and you have to be prepared and armored every day for that moment. But even spiritual Rambos need a home team to retreat to for healing, supplies, and encouragement.

I'm talking about two things here—Christian friends and a good church.

Christian friends are super important. This doesn't mean

you have to dump all your non-Christian friends. In fact, I think that would be a huge mistake. But you do need to be aware that who you spend time with affects you. The apostle Paul wrote: "Do not be deceived: 'Bad company corrupts good morals'" (1 Corinthians 15:33).

Find some people who love Jesus at least as much as you do. These are your fellow travelers on the narrow road. These are your true soul mates, your spiritual brothers and sisters. When you date, be sure you're dating people who love Jesus at least as much as you do.

There's nothing like walking through life with someone who is going the same direction you are, who has the same master you have, and who will spur you on to "love and good deeds" (Hebrews 10:24). These are the people you have the most in common with. They're your home team.

You also need to be in a good church. Sometimes people like to get out of this. They say they don't buy into organized religion. My comeback to that is a line from the movie *Sneakers:* "Don't kid yourself: It's not that organized."

What's a church good for?

Sure, it might be where you find like-minded friends or even a prospective marriage partner. But it's also the place you come to get fed and be encouraged. It's where you can learn the Bible and the Christian worldview. If it's a good, Bible-teaching church, you'll get challenged and strengthened every week.

It's also the place to use your gifts. God gave you a spiritual gift (maybe more than one) when you became a Christian. He gives out those gifts for the primary reason of being used in the local church (see Romans 12 and 1 Corinthians 14).

The best reason to be faithful and active in your local church is that the Bible commands it (Hebrews 10:25). If you've really jumped off the fence in the direction of Jesus, then you'll want to do what He asks just because He asks it. It's not an act of blind obedience to avoid being crushed by a vengeful Judge; it's a joyful rush to delight the One who gave His all that you might have eternal life.

You gotta be part of a strong home team.

Phase 3: Lost People in Your Circle

When you've got your soul centered on Jesus in your quiet time and you've got the support of your Christian friends and church, you're finally ready to begin going out to the lost world. But you don't need to head out to deepest, darkest Africa just yet. Maybe someday, but not right away.

Why? Because God has put you right where you are for a reason. The people in your circle—your friends, family, classmates, and coworkers—are your own personal mission field. Imagine God looking down on the world and thinking, *Okay, I need somebody who can reach all these folks in this area here. Hmm…. Oh, I know! I'll put* this one *right in the middle of them.* You are the one God has strategically placed in your circle of influence to be His ambassador and servant. Like the old saying goes, you are the only Bible some people will ever read.

In that circle of yours, there are bound to be some people who don't follow Jesus with all their heart. Some are probably atheists, some might be members of a bizarre cult, some might just be clueless. I'm betting that you even know a few moral relativists—otherwise you wouldn't have picked up this book. These are the folks God wants to influence through you.

Don't get me wrong: I don't think you have to go blow these people away with the Bible. The double-barreled shotgun approach isn't going to do anybody any good. That's being intolerant, all right, but not in love. Your heart might be in the right place, but your actions may just offend these people so badly that you actually push them *away* from Christ. You're not warning them away from the collapsed bridge, you're getting behind them and pushing them over it.

There is a time and place for direct confrontation. But even then it's got to be wrapped in love.

Being Lovingly Intolerant to Lost People in Your Circle

There's a guy I used to go to church with. We'll call him Dave. Dave went through a nasty divorce. After that, he started sleeping with any woman with two feet and a heartbeat who would have him. I realized that it was time for me to be intolerant—in love.

I pulled him aside one day. "Dude," I said, "what are you doing?"

"Aw, Ryan, I'm just getting a little, you know. Having some fun."

"Dave, you can't do that."

"What are you talking about, man? Stay out of my business."

"No, Dave, what you're doing is wrong. It's sin, bro. You're going against God's Word. And to be coming to church and professing to be a Christian and doing that? Dude, you're giving us a bad name. Are you telling these girls you go to church? Is that the line you use with them, that you're this great godly guy? You gotta cut it out."

He wouldn't look me in the eye. He just stared at his feet. "I know, man. It's just…so difficult, you know? I hate being divorced. I miss the sex. I miss feeling that way with somebody."

What do you think? Was I intolerant toward Dave? You bet. Did I condemn him and blow him apart with the

Bible? No. I took a stand, *in love,* to try to get a friend back on the right path. He knew I was right, but it took someone actually saying something to him to make him admit it.

I'll bet you've got people all around you who are like Dave. Good people doing stupid things, things that are only going to make them miserable and lead to disaster. The moral relativist will most likely either condemn them as horrible people or wink at their actions. If those are your only two choices, you've got a real problem. But, praise Jesus, there *is* another option: You can gently, lovingly, and with great compassion show these people another way.

This is how Paul says the Christian should react to lost people around him: "Those who oppose him he must gently instruct, in the hope that God will grant them repentance leading them to a knowledge of the truth" (2 Timothy 2:25, NIV).

If you unload both barrels on your lost friend or family member, you're not likely to get very far. If you keep your mouth shut, you're an accomplice to his eternal death. *But,* if you can take this person aside and show him that you love him and want the best for him, he's likely to listen. My non-Christian friends listen to me because I've taken the time to listen to them and invest in their lives. They know I care, so they're willing to listen when their world comes crashing down and their philosophy abandons them in their moment of need.

Are there lost people around you who don't hear about your faith because you're afraid of losing their friendship? Maybe they're clients at work or some popular girls on campus. You want these people to like you, and you're pretty sure that if you said what they were doing was wrong, they wouldn't like you anymore.

If that's you, then I've got to challenge you again: Are you going to be a man pleaser or a God pleaser (Galatians 1:10)? Do you care more about what some people think of you than what God thinks about you? Are you here to fit in with their plan or with His?

Think about this: You don't know when these people are going to die. They could get into a car today and be killed on the way home. Did they ever hear about Jesus? God has put *you* in their lives to be His ambassador. You're His megaphone, through which He wants to call out to them to come to Him and be saved.

I ask you: Is it more loving to leave these people in their sin or to find a way to gently tell them what you believe and why?

Jesus spent a ton of time with unbelievers.
He was constantly being slammed because of how much time He spent with prostitutes, dishonest tax collectors, and other undesirables. That's why I don't cut myself off from my non-Christian friends. If we don't ever talk to non-Christians, how can

anyone be saved? How could you or I have ever been saved if no one talked to non-Christians?

The key is not letting them influence you. You want to influence them, but you can't allow them to influence you, not on spiritual matters. It's like that statement from Paul: Bad company will corrupt good morals. If you find yourself so close to a lost person that he or she is having influence over you in spiritual matters, you've got to step away.

I have another friend. Let's call him Mike. I've known Mike since I was ten. We were in Boy Scouts together. If you were ever in a crisis situation, Mike could get you out. And believe me, I was in a lot of those situations.

Mike was the go-to guy for everything. He's a paramedic, he's got a photographic memory, he's a contractor, he's a mechanic, he's an Eagle Scout. If you ever needed something built, fixed, or bandaged, he was the guy. If a fight broke out, he would have your back. Once we were together and a guy pulled a gun on us. Mike rushed the gunman. If you were low on money, he'd be there for you. He was just one of those guys.

He was totally clean, too.

But then…Mike started making up for lost time. He had never even smoked pot until he was thirty years old. I don't know what it was, but he just went off the deep end. Drugs, booze, sex with anybody. It was totally weird. I

HOW TO BE INTOLERANT—IN LOVE | **105**

mean, I had known the guy practically all my life. He had tremendous influence over me.

But when he did all that, I had to pull away. I don't talk to Mike anymore, even today. We don't hang around together. And that's very strange for me. It really bothers him that I don't listen to his advice. When he calls and wants to have a serious conversation with me about what I should do, I don't listen to him because his world is consumed with alcohol and marijuana now.

It hurts us both that we can't be friends, but Mike doesn't get it. It finally came down to the question of who was influencing whom. Was I pulling him up or was he pulling me down? When I realized he was pulling me down, I had to get away from him. Sometimes you have to ask yourself if your friends are really the people you want to have as your friends.

I still love Mike. I still pray for him. I still lovingly confront him in my words and actions. But I don't let him have influence over me anymore.

What about you? Do you have a Mike in your life? Somebody who is living contrary to the way you know Jesus wants you to live? If so, you've got to confront him or her, in love. If that person blows you off, then you've got to step away. Otherwise he or she is going to lead you off the narrow path and back onto the road that leads to destruction. The road with the bridge out.

When your friends want to go do something you know you shouldn't be doing, don't go. If you're not sure about it, the thing that should swing your decision is if you'll be making a Christlike difference in their lives and whether or not you'll be sinning if you go. If you're there to influence them toward Christ and it won't drag you into sin, then maybe you go. But if you're just there to party with them and you're blowing your reputation as a Christian, you just can't do it.

Jesus hung around with the "evildoers" of the day, but He didn't sin with them. He reached out to them to bring them to God, but He was separate from their sin.

This is what it looks like to be lovingly intolerant to your non-Christian friends—or to your Christian friends who are straying from the straight and narrow. You take a stand, gently, because of who you are and *whose* you are. That's why it's so vital to get Phases 1 and 2 down. You've got to be rooted in your time with God and with a group of Christians who can prop you up. It's a nasty world out there and it's very unpopular to say that sin is sin, even if you do so in love.

Jesus didn't come to unite the world in perfect harmony, but to divide it (Matthew 10:34–36). You gotta jump to one side of the line or the other.

If you stand up to what your lost friends and family are doing, I want to warn you that it won't always have a happy ending. **Sometimes you'll actually end up standing alone.** On a human level, at least. But you'll never *really* be standing alone when you're speaking the truth in love. What they're turning away from isn't you, but God: "He who rejects this instruction does not reject man but God, who gives you his Holy Spirit" (1 Thessalonians 4:8, NIV).

And if they turn away from God, then they're choosing to go on over the broken bridge. They've stopped to hear your warning, but they've decided that's what they want to do anyway. At that point, all you can do is pray for them.

> When the watchman sees the enemy coming, he
> blows the alarm to warn the people. Then if those
> who hear the alarm refuse to take action—well, it is
> their own fault if they die. They heard the warning
> but wouldn't listen, so the responsibility is theirs. If
> they had listened to the warning, they could have
> saved their lives. But if the watchman sees the
> enemy coming and doesn't sound the alarm to warn
> the people, he is responsible for their deaths. They
> will die in their sins, but I will hold the watchman
> accountable.
>
> EZEKIEL 33:3–6, NLT

Phase 4: Going out into the World

Here's when you might head off to Africa. You've got your
armor on from your time with Jesus, you've got godly
friends and a Bible-teaching church, and you've gently
taken the non-Christians in your circle aside to show
them a better way. What's left? The world, baby.

But don't be too quick to start learning Swahili. God
may still want you to impact the corner of the world where
He put you. The Bible tells us that God decided when,
where, and to whom you would be born (Acts 17:25–27).
This is more of His strategic plan. If He'd wanted you to
impact Africa, He might very well have decided you should
be born there. I'm not dissing missionary work at all, I just
think that unless we have a very clear call from God to go
somewhere else, we should stay right where we are.

Jesus said that people like you and me are the light of
the world (Matthew 5:14). If we don't let that light shine,
we doom our nation to darkness. He also said we're the salt
of the earth (v. 13). One of the things salt was used for in
that day was to preserve meat from spoiling. If we keep the
truth to ourselves, our culture will rot.

We're the only thing holding off the decay in the first place.

Do I mean go become a pro-life activist? Not
necessarily. If God calls you to that, fine. But you have to be

sure you're making that kind of a stand with lots of love, or you'll just look like one more crazy radical whose only difference from the people on the other side of the picket line is the slogan on your sign.

How can you be intolerant in love on the larger stage? You do it by taking a loving but firm stand for biblical values, no matter the cost. I see it when I go speak for Crisis Pregnancy Centers. These people put their hearts on the line every day talking to pregnant moms who are about to abort their babies. **These people are trying to save lives.**

I see it in my friend, Sid, a tattoo artist. He is a great, great Christian man who started a Bible study for a bunch of skaters. They read a few chapters of the New Testament every day and get together once a week and talk about it. Sid makes a difference in people's lives. He cares. He prays.

I see it in Rob, who works with Sid. Rob used to be a gangbanger. He has some really scary tattoos. But now he's just overcome with the Spirit. He and his wife are raising a niece to take her out of a bad situation. He's teaching this little girl the ways of the Lord.

I see it in my dad, who takes a stand on a daily basis no matter what anybody says. He does what God wants him to do, even though people don't like it. A *lot* of people. They put him down and they take him off the air because he makes a stand for Christ. And he does it anyway. He could take the easy way out. When he was on the gambling and pornography commission, we got threats from the Mafia. He could have said, "You know what? Enough of this." But he did what God wanted him to do.

I see the loving intolerance of Christ in the lone high school student who stands at the flagpole and prays on See You at the Pole Day, even though no one else shows up. Kids make fun of him for having a Bible and for doing a Bible study. They call him "Jesus freak." But he does it anyway. Because he is popular for it? **No, because it's right; it's what God told him to do.**

I see this kind of loving intolerance in my friend Christianne, who is going to get all of us into heaven if she can. She does what's right, no matter what people think. She doesn't get asked out on a regular basis, but she'll drop everything when you're in trouble and in need. She goes and prays for people. She calls and says, "I was thinking about you today."

I see it in my friend Jamie, a beautiful young girl who wasn't asked out a single time during her high school years. Why? Because she was and is doing what God wants her to do. She takes a stand. She does the uncomfortable thing. When her roommate was sleeping with her boyfriend, she said, "Girl, what you're doing is wrong."

That is what it looks like to stand for Christ in a

morally relativistic world. Can you do this kind of thing, too? Absolutely! And you know what? *You have to.* God has placed you right where you are and in just this time in human history because He needs you to stand up for truth. He needs people standing beside the wide, well-traveled interstate, lobbing flares at motorists who are headed for their deaths but don't know it.

Phase 5: Back to the Prayer Closet

The world can beat you up. Even with your armor on and your home team all around you, if you take a stand for truth you will sometimes have abuse heaped on you. That's when you have to run back to Jesus.

There's an old song by Twila Paris called "The Warrior Is a Child." In the song she says that everybody sees her as strong and brave and always at the front of the battle. What no one sees is that every day she goes crawling back to God, who picks her up and just lets her cry. Because He's there for her, tomorrow she can go back out and fight again.

You and I are warrior-children, too. Nobody likes being told they're wrong. Your friends and family won't. The moral relativists in America sure won't. It doesn't matter how gentle and loving you are, in the end they know you're saying they're wrong. And that's intolerant.

Yes, frankly, it is. But it's right. And it's loving. And it's their only hope for avoiding the broken bridge.

On your own, you can't fight this fight. Not even one day. You need armor. Better yet, how about an armored fortress?

- "The name of the LORD is a strong tower; the righteous runs into it and is safe" (Proverbs 18:10).
- "The LORD is my rock, my fortress and my deliverer; my God is my rock, in whom I take refuge, my shield and the horn of my salvation. He is my stronghold, my refuge and my savior—from violent men you save me" (2 Samuel 22:2–3, NIV).
- "He is my loving God and my fortress, my stronghold and my deliverer, my shield, in whom I take refuge, who subdues peoples under me" (Psalm 144:2, NIV).

And one more great one to send you out with:

Do not be afraid of the terrors of the night, nor fear the dangers of the day, nor dread the plague that stalks in darkness, nor the disaster that strikes at midday. Though a thousand fall at your side, though ten thousand are dying around you, these evils will not touch you.... If you make the LORD your refuge, if you make the Most High your shelter, no evil will conquer you; no plague will come near your dwelling.

PSALM 91:5–7, 9–10, NLT

Now get on into that prayer closet, and onto your home team! Then head out to the completely blind world, your flare gun at your side.

And be intolerant—in love.

Conclusion

★ ★ ★ ★ ★

MEN WANTED: FOR HAZARDOUS JOURNEY.
SMALL WAGES, BITTER COLD, LONG MONTHS
OF COMPLETE DARKNESS, CONSTANT DANGER,
SAFE RETURN DOUBTFUL. HONOUR AND
RECOGNITION IN CASE OF SUCCESS.[8]

Sound like fun? Ready to sign up? This is the recruitment ad that Irish-born explorer Sir Ernest Shackleton reportedly ran in 1914 to gather a crew for his expedition to cross the Antarctic continent. Believe it or not, twenty-seven people signed up. They answered Shackleton's call, even knowing the hardships and dangers they would certainly face.

Jesus makes a similar call to you and me:

"If any of you wants to be my follower, you must put aside your selfish ambition, shoulder your cross daily, and follow me. If you try to keep your life for yourself, you will lose it. But if you give up your life for me, you will find true life. And how do you benefit if you gain the whole world but lose or forfeit your own soul in the process? If a person is ashamed of me and my message, I, the Son of Man, will be ashamed of that person when I return in my glory and in the glory of the Father and the holy angels."

LUKE 9:23–26, NLT

Both expeditions offer the adventure of a lifetime. Both are full of danger and hardship. Both offer amazing rewards to those who complete the journey. And both groups will be led by the person who is making the call. He'll be there facing whatever you face, offering guidance and expert counsel. You won't be alone, even though you will be set apart.

Are you up for that kind of adventure? Are you ready to join Jesus and follow Him all the way?

I can't promise you a safe ride. I can't promise you an easy life. What I *can* promise is that in this life you will have trials and tribulations. There will be hard, hard times. There will be high highs and low lows. But now you will finally have purpose and meaning. It just doesn't get more exciting than that. If you're ready for that kind of living, then welcome to the adventure!

Mission Accomplished?

In the beginning I said I had one goal for this book: to take you from trying to be an "inclusive, open-minded Christian" who doesn't get persecuted or make anyone mad and lead you to a courageous walk with Jesus Christ that makes you willing to gently but firmly stand up for what is biblical, true, and right.

So, how'd I do? When people demand that you accept their homosexuality, are you not quite as intimidated when you realize how miserable they really are? Does it strike you as hypocritical now when you're shouted down for being intolerant? Do you have a good argument prepared for the next time people say they don't believe in absolute truth?

Moral relativism is a TUMOR on the American soul.

It's a wonderful philosophy if all you want to do is defy Christianity, as Satan surely does. The problem is that when you get off the narrow road that Jesus has marked out, you end up in meaninglessness and depression. And you could end up in slavery.

I saw a great quote at the end of a Bruce Willis movie, *Tears of the Sun*. The quote was by Edmund Burke, a political philosopher who lived in the eighteenth century: "The only thing necessary for the triumph of evil is for good men to do nothing."

Think about that. Christians are the only thing holding back the decay of our world. If Satan can make us dump the Bible and live by a philosophy that says it's wrong to stand up to evil—or even to call anything evil—then we're all set up for the rise of a great world tyrant. The Bible calls him the Antichrist.

It takes courage to stand up for Jesus and biblical values in today's world. If you do that, you may be heckled and abused. But you know what? It doesn't matter. Because pleasing God and displeasing man will make Judgment Day a whole lot better for you than if you'd spent your life pleasing man and displeasing God.

The End

I'm intolerant. I'm not ignorant, but I am intolerant. I'm not a racist or a bigot, but I am intolerant. I don't hate people; I disagree with ideas. Make no mistake, I am intolerant.

I am intolerant because I love. The world hates me because I love in this way, but I cannot stop. I dare not stop. I serve a Lord who loved enough to be intolerant. The world hated Him, too. If I say I follow Him, I have to do what He did.

"If the world hates you, keep in mind that it hated me first. If you belonged to the world, it would love you as its own. As it is, you do not belong to the world, but I have chosen you out of the world. That is why the world hates you. Remember the words I spoke to you: 'No servant is greater than his master.' If they persecuted me, they will persecute you also. If they obeyed my teaching, they will obey yours also. They will treat you this way because of my name, for they do not know the One who sent me."

JOHN 15:18–21, NIV

Jesus isn't one of the ways to get to the Father. He's the *only* way. If you would follow Him, you have to get in the fight. No more trying to please the world and please God at the same time. Get your armor on, take up your cross, and come on out to where the adventure begins.

Go out and be intolerant—in love.

The publisher and author would love to hear your comments about this book.
Please contact us at:
www.multnomah.net/ryandobson

★ ★ ★ ★ ★

Notes

1. Charles Colson, "It's Not My Fault," *BreakPoint Online,* 22
    August 2002. http://www.breakpoint.org/Breakpoint/
    ChannelRoot/FeaturesGroup/BreakPointCommentaries/Its+Not+
    My+Fault.htm (accessed 19 May 2003).
2. Peter Stoner, *Science Speaks* (The Moody Bible Institute of
    Chicago, 1963), 106–07.
3. Josh McDowell, *Evidence That Demands a Verdict* (Here's Life
    Publishers, Inc.: San Bernadino, Calif., 1979), 111–2.
4. As quoted by C. S. Lewis in Josh McDowell, *Evidence That
    Demands a Verdict* (Here's Life Publishers, Inc.: San Bernadino,
    Calif., 1979), 103–7.
5. Ibid, 103.
6. As quoted by Peter Schaff in Josh McDowell, *Evidence That
    Demands a Verdict* (Here's Life Publishers, Inc.: San Bernadino,
    Calif., 1979), 107.
7. "Bridge rescuer credits 'greater power than us,'" *CNN.com,* 28
    May 2002. http://www.cnn.com/2002/US/05/28/
    barton.cnna/index.html (accessed 19 May 2003). "Bridge
    Recovery Work Yields 14 Bodies," *FoxNews.com,* 29 May 2002.
    http://www.foxnews.com/story/0,2933,53898,00.html (accessed
    19 May 2003).
8. "Shackleton's Voyage of Endurance," *NOVA Online,* 10 April
    2000. http://www.pbs.org/wgbh/nova/shacklcton/
    dispatches/20000410.html (accessed 23 May 2003).